FINDING YOUR EXIT DOOR

RECLAIM YOUR JOURNEY, LIVE WITH FAITH, AND STEP INTO YOUR TRUE PURPOSE

NAYE LIGGINES

Copyright © 2024 by *Ebone Liggines*

All rights reserved.

No part of this book may be reproduced, distributed, or transmitted in any form or by any means, including photocopying, recording, or other electronic or mechanical methods, without the prior written permission of the publisher, except in the case of brief quotations embodied in critical reviews and certain other noncommercial uses permitted by copyright law.

This is a work of fiction. Names, characters, places, and incidents are either the product of the author's imagination or used fictitiously. Any resemblance to actual persons, living or dead, events, or locales is purely coincidental.

Published by *Elevation Talks*

www.elevationtalks.com

ISBN: *979-8-218-56427-8*

Cover Design by *Nabin Karna*

Table of Contents

Dedication v
Acknowledgments vi
Preface viii
CHAPTER 1: Recognizing Life's Limitations - Breaking Mental Chains 1
CHAPTER 2: Letting Go of What No Longer Serves You - Releasing the Old, Embracing the New 11
CHAPTER 3: Relationships & Self-Worth - The Heart of Our Journey 21
CHAPTER 4: The Courage to Step Away - Your Path to the Exit Door 31
CHAPTER 5: Embracing Change - Riding the Waves of Change 41
CHAPTER 6: The Exit Door Unveiled - Crossing the Threshold 51
CHAPTER 7: Rewriting Your Life's Narrative - Authoring Your Future 61
CHAPTER 8: Setting Goals for Your Dream Life 71
CHAPTER 9: Living Your Dream Life - The Essence of Fulfillment 81
CHAPTER 10: Beyond the Exit Door – Reflecting on Your Journey 91
Beyond the Exit Door 99

Dedication

Dear Heavenly Father,

This book is for You.

Thank You for trusting me to speak to Your people and for planting the vision for this book in my heart. When You first called me to write it, I resisted. I told You I wasn't an author and didn't believe I could do it. But even as I wrestled with self-doubt and tried to ignore the call, You didn't let me go. You saw something in me that I couldn't see in myself.

Thank You for Your patience and for never giving up on me, even when I doubted myself. Thank You for being my strength when I was weak, for guiding me when I felt lost, and for constantly reminding me that I am capable because of You.

This book isn't just the result of my work—it's a reflection of Your faithfulness. I'm so grateful for the gifts and creativity You've blessed me with and for pushing me to use them for Your glory. I know this isn't the only book You've called me to write, and I trust that You will continue to guide me every step of the way.

I love You, Lord, and I thank You for believing in me when I didn't believe in myself. Without You, none of this would have been possible.

Acknowledgments

To my mom—LOL—you never really understand what I do, but you always try to show up in your own way, and I love you so much for that. Thank you for showing up for me, even when it wasn't easy, and for making sacrifices that I may not have always fully appreciated at the time. I know that your own dreams were cut short in so many ways, and my heart aches for the things you had to let go of. But I also pray that as you see me walking in the dreams God gave me, you'll be inspired to ask Him to restore your dreams, too.

You still have so much life left to live, and I believe with my whole heart that God isn't finished with you yet. Thank you for everything you've done for me and for the way you've loved me, even in the ways you didn't know how. I pray that you find healing, joy, and the courage to dream again because you deserve it. I love you endlessly, and I'm so grateful for you.

To my dad—thank you for always seeing me, for loving me, and for accepting me fully, even past my sexuality. You've never looked at me any differently, and that means more to me than I could ever express.

To my auntie—thank you so much for pouring into me the way you do. Sometimes we'll talk, and I can feel God speaking through you just to get to me. You told me once, "If you keep being stubborn, you're going to keep talking to the same mountain." And you'll never know how much that meant to me. Every conversation we have lifts me up, fills me, and reminds me of the incredible women I'm surrounded by. I love laughing with you, learning from you, and hearing you come from a place of understanding and interest—it's almost like we're the same person! Thank you for constantly encouraging me to open up the Word, to let God use me, and to stay connected to His voice. You've been such a blessing in my life, and I appreciate you more than words can say.

To my grandfather—you were the greatest example of what a leader, a man of God, and a man of faith should look like. Thank you for praying for us as a family, for guiding us, and for leading with love and grace. Watching your light shine and touch so many people was an honor. I'm so proud to have called you my grandfather, and I'm so grateful for the lessons you taught us just by being who you were.

To my oldest brother—thank you for never shutting down my dreams, even though yours were shut down. You've always been there for me, always been my partner in crime when I needed you to be. I pray that when you're ready, you take everything you've been holding and lay it at God's feet, trusting Him to change your life the way only He can.

To my dear friend—you know who you are. From day one, you've been in my corner, cheering me on. Before I even started writing this book, you invested in me—literally—and gave me $20 to get started. That simple gesture meant the world to me, and it was a spark that lit the fire to make this book a reality. I'm so grateful for your support, your belief in me, and your friendship.

To everyone else who has been part of my journey—you've been here, walking with me, encouraging me, and lifting me up when I needed it most. I'm so blessed to have such dope people in my life, people who not only believe in me but also continue to ride with me as I grow into who God created me to be. I love each and every one of you, and I pray that God continues to pour into all of our lives, filling us with overflow, blessings, and His divine presence.

In Jesus' name—Amen!

Preface

AYOOO! What it do?!

First off, let me tell you how this whole idea of **"Finding Your Exit Door"** came to be. You might be sitting there wondering, "What is this even about?" But trust me, this is about to hit different. It all started back in January 2023 when I was fasting and praying. During that time, I wasn't expecting much—just trying to get closer to God, do some reflection, you know? But then, out of nowhere, *BOOM*—God hit me with this vision to write a book.

The message? **It's time to leave behind the things that aren't helping you grow anymore.** Whether that's a dead-end job, a toxic relationship, or just a mindset that's keeping you stuck. If you've ever felt like you're just *going through the motions*, waking up every day wondering, "Is this it?"—you're not alone. I've been there. And that's exactly what this book is about. It's about finding your own exit door, that next step toward what God's calling you to do.

See, back then, I didn't even know I was about to hit a rough patch. I had no idea that I was about to go through my own exit door. My job was something I used to be proud of—it felt like my thing, you know? I was a video producer for this big phone accessories brand, working with top brands, directing, filming, the whole nine yards. I loved it. I never woke up dreading going to work. But man...there came a point where it just didn't feel right anymore. Something was off.

I started feeling trapped, and deep down, I knew it was time to bounce. But let me be real with you—I was scared. Scared because I didn't have a Plan B. I didn't have a fat savings account to fall back on. And honestly? I had a bunch of reasons to stay comfortable.

One day, at work, we got these motivational posters. My coworker thought it would be fun if we picked them randomly. I ended up with one that said, **"If it doesn't challenge you, it won't change you."** And I slapped that on my desk without thinking too much about it. But man, as time went by, those words started to hit home *hard*. I realized I was way too comfortable. Nothing in my life was pushing me anymore, and because of that, I wasn't growing.

That's when I started looking at my situation differently. I looked at all the PTO I hadn't used—over 100 hours just sitting there, untouched. It was like I had pressed *pause* on living my life because of this job. And one day, as I sat there thinking about all this, I noticed the exit sign above the door flicker. You know the red exit signs that be above the doors? Yeah, one of those. And as I looked up, I saw the door was wide open, sunlight pouring through, lighting up the path. It was like God was telling me, **"Yo, it's time to move on!"**

That was my sign. Literally.

From that moment, I knew God was calling me to something bigger. I started to reflect on what He'd been planting in my heart for a while—visions of me on stage, at places like Transformation Church, speaking to people, and writing books. But I laughed it off at first. I told God, "You sure, Lord? I'm no speaker. I barely speak proper English! Ain't nobody tryna hear me." But God kept nudging me, showing me that I didn't need to be perfect. I just needed to be *faithful*.

I felt so burnt out from work, and I told God, "I don't have time for what you've called me to do." And y'all, I promise God has a sense of humor. A little while after that, I got laid off. At first, I was shook. But then it hit me—God wasn't punishing me; He was clearing my schedule so I could make space for my dreams.

That layoff was scary, but it forced me to lean into my faith like never before. I started making more motivational videos, pouring my heart and soul into them, because honestly, it was the only thing that made me feel alive at that point.

This book is not just about me or my struggles. It's about **you**. It's about giving you the tools to find your own exit door, to leave behind what's been holding you back, and step into a new season of your life—one that's full of purpose, faith, and growth. So, are you ready? Ready to kick open that door and step into the life God has for you?

Welcome to *Finding Your Exit Door*.

As we go through these pages, keep your eyes on that exit door. Let it be your guide through the ups and downs, the victories and the struggles. But before we dive deep, I've got some questions for you. This ain't just a book—it's a guide for real transformation. When you answer these questions, you're not just jotting down some words. You're laying out your path from where you are to where you're supposed to be.

Don't rush. Take your time. Be real with yourself. Grab a journal if you need to. This is about figuring out where you're standing right now and where God wants you to go.

Ready? Let's go find that door.

1. Reflect on Your Hallway: Consider the different 'doors' in your life. Which ones have been difficult to close or leave behind? Are there any doors you're curious to open but haven't yet?

2. Focus and Direction: Are you more fixated on the past (the doors behind you) or the future (the doors ahead)? How is this focus influencing your journey?

CHAPTER 1:

Recognizing Life's Limitations - Breaking Mental Chains

Ayo, let's get real for a second. This journey we're on? It starts right here, with the mind. The way you think shapes everything—your choices, your opportunities, and the doors you'll either walk through or stay locked behind. So, the first step on this journey is simple, but it ain't easy. We gotta break free from the mental chains that have been holding us back.

You know what I'm talking about—those limiting beliefs, that negative self-talk, the doubt that whispers, "You can't do this. You're not enough." Yeah, we all deal with it, but the truth is, you're more powerful than you think.

Take Yazmen, for example. She's one of those people who's always had big dreams—ever since she was a kid. But everyone around her, from her friends to her family, kept telling her, **"That's not for people like us."** And over time, those voices became her own. The world told her she couldn't, and eventually, she believed it. It's crazy how that happens, right?

Yazmen's life became this endless cycle of *what ifs* and *if onlys*. She watched her friends settle into jobs and lives that didn't bring them any joy, and she started doing the same. But deep down, she was restless. There was this fire in her soul, but it felt like she didn't know how to fan the flames. She was stuck.

Then one night, something clicked. She had this moment of clarity, like God had been trying to speak to her, and for the first time, she actually listened. It wasn't about what other people thought anymore. It was about that voice inside of her that had been quietly saying, "Yes, you can."

In that moment, she realized something: **the voices that matter aren't the ones telling you no—they're the ones whispering yes.** And more often than not, that voice is God, planting dreams in your heart, telling you it's time to step into something new. It's time to break free.

Yazmen didn't just wake up the next morning and have everything figured out, but she started making moves. She let go of the limiting beliefs that had been placed on her. She stopped asking people for permission to live the life God was calling her to. And the more she stepped out in faith, the more those mental chains fell off.

Here's what Yazmen's story teaches us: **the mind is where the battle is won or lost**. If you keep telling yourself you're not enough, that you're stuck, that this is all there is—then guess what? That's what your reality will look like. But if you start flipping those thoughts, start telling yourself you can do this, you are capable, you are worthy of what God has for you—then you'll begin to see things shift.

Breaking Free from Limiting Beliefs

So, here's the real question: **What beliefs are holding you back?** Take a moment. Think about it. What stories have you been telling yourself that are keeping you stuck in place? And more importantly, how are you going to flip those thoughts?

It all starts with recognizing that you *can* change the narrative in your head. You're not a prisoner to those old beliefs. You have the power to rewrite the story.

Here's how:

1. **Challenge those beliefs.** When the thought pops up that says, "I can't," ask yourself, "Who says I can't? Where did that thought come from?" Nine times out of ten, it's coming from fear, not truth.
2. **Replace the negative with positive.** Speak life into yourself. When you catch yourself thinking negatively, replace it with something positive. Instead of, "I'll never make it," say, "I'm on the path to something great."

3. **Stay grounded in faith.** Trust that God didn't plant dreams in your heart just to leave you hanging. If He's called you to it, He's already equipped you to do it. Lean on Him when doubt creeps in.
4. **Surround yourself with the right people.** The company you keep will either help you break those mental chains or keep you bound. Be around people who see your potential and speak life into you.
5. **Celebrate the small wins.** Every step forward, no matter how small, is progress. You're breaking free little by little. Don't forget to celebrate that.

Before we move forward, let me ask you this:

1. Identifying Mental Chains: What beliefs or fears are currently holding you back? Be honest with yourself. Write them down.

_____

_____

_____

_____

_____

_____

_____

_____

_____

_____

_____

_____

_____

_____

_____

_____

_____

_____

_____

2. Understanding Stagnation: Where in your life do you feel stuck? How has this impacted your dreams or goals?

_____
_____
_____
_____
_____
_____
_____
_____
_____
_____
_____
_____
_____
_____
_____
_____
_____

3. Taking Action: What's one step you can take this week to start breaking those mental chains? Maybe it's speaking a positive affirmation, maybe it's reaching out to someone for support—whatever it is, write it down and do it.

Closing Thoughts

Yazmen's story shows us that breaking free isn't about having all the answers. It's about taking that first step in faith, trusting that God has more for you than what you're currently experiencing. You're not stuck unless you choose to be. So, what's it gonna be? Are you ready to start breaking those mental chains and walking through your exit door?

Moving Forward

Breaking free from the mental chains that hold you back is the first step to reclaiming your journey, but it's only the beginning. Recognizing the limitations is one thing—now it's time to start letting go of the things that no longer serve you.

In the next chapter, we'll explore the art of letting go—releasing the habits, fears, and relationships that are keeping you stuck so you can make space for the life God is calling you to step into. Let's keep moving forward.

CHAPTER 2:

Letting Go of What No Longer Serves You - Releasing the Old, Embracing the New

This chapter is all about letting go. You know what I'm talking about—those things in your life that you've been holding onto for way too long. Maybe it's a job, a relationship, a habit, or even a mindset that isn't serving you anymore. But here's the thing: **you can't step into your future if your hands are full of the past**.

I get it. Letting go is tough. We cling to what's familiar because it feels safe—even when it's draining us, even when it's not leading us anywhere. But here's the truth: **sometimes the very things we're afraid to let go of are the very things that are keeping us from the life God wants for us**.

Let's talk about my boy, Tommy. Now, Tommy grew up in a family where tradition was everything. Everyone followed a certain path: get a stable job, settle down, play it safe. Tommy? He had different dreams, but he ignored them for years because he didn't want to rock the boat. He had a job that paid well, his family approved, and from the outside looking in, everything seemed good. But deep down, Tommy was miserable.

He kept telling himself that he *should* be happy—he had the paycheck, the stability, and the approval of his family. But every day felt like a slow grind, a series of moments where he was just going through the motions. It was like wearing a mask that didn't fit anymore. Tommy was suffocating, but he didn't want to disappoint anyone by taking it off.

Then, one random Tuesday, Tommy hit a breaking point. He was sitting in his office, staring out the window, and he realized something: **this life wasn't his.** He was living someone else's script, and it was time to write his own. In that moment, Tommy made a decision to let go of everything that wasn't true to him.

It wasn't easy. He had to leave behind a job that everyone else thought was "perfect" for him. He had to deal with the questions and the disapproval from people he loved. But for the first time in a long time, Tommy felt free. He wasn't living for other people anymore—he was living for **himself** and, more importantly, for **the life God was calling him to.**

Tommy's story hits because we've all been there, haven't we? We've all clung to things that we *think* we need, even when they're not making us happy, even when they're keeping us stuck. It's like holding onto an old pair of shoes that used to fit, but now they're just giving you blisters. You're scared to throw them away because they used to be your favorite, but now? **They don't fit the life you're meant to walk into anymore.**

God has something better for you, but to receive it, you've gotta let go of what's not meant for you anymore. You've gotta trust that what's ahead is better than what's behind.

The Art of Letting Go

Letting go isn't just about walking away from something; it's about **making space for the new**. When you let go of the old, you make room for God to bring in new opportunities, new people, new experiences that are meant to help you grow.

So, what are you holding onto right now that's not serving you? Is it a job that feels like it's draining your soul? Is it a relationship where you're the only one putting in the effort? Is it a mindset that's keeping you playing small, afraid to step into the unknown?

Here's how we start the process of letting go:

1. **Acknowledge What's No Longer Working.** Be honest with yourself. What's that one thing in your life that you've been holding onto, even though you know it's not leading you where you need to go? A job? A relationship? A habit? Write it down.

2. **Trust God's Timing.** God didn't put you on this earth to live a mediocre life. If He's asking you to let something go, it's because He's got something better in store. Trust in His timing. You might not see the new thing yet, but you've gotta let go of the old to make room for it.
3. **Face Your Fear of Change.** Let's be real—most of the time, it's not the thing itself that's hard to let go of; it's the **fear** of what happens next. What if you quit your job and the new one doesn't come? What if you leave the relationship and end up alone? That fear of the unknown is what keeps us stuck. But here's the truth: **God can't steer a parked car.** You've gotta move, trust Him, and know He's got the next step ready for you.
4. **Surround Yourself with Support.** Letting go is easier when you've got people in your corner. Talk to friends, mentors, or people you trust. Let them know what you're going through. Sometimes all it takes is someone else reminding you of your worth and your calling to help you take that leap.
5. **Make the Decision and Don't Look Back.** Once you've made the decision to let go, don't second-guess it. Don't keep revisiting what could have been. The moment you start looking backward, you stop moving forward. Trust that God's got this. What's behind you is done. It's time to step forward into what's next.

Why Letting Go is Necessary for Growth

Here's what I need you to know: **letting go isn't about losing—it's about gaining**. When you let go of something that's been holding you back, you gain freedom. You gain space for something better. You gain clarity on what truly matters to you.

Think about it this way: if your hands are full, you can't receive anything new. You've gotta release what's weighing you down before you can take hold of the blessings God is trying to give you.

In Tommy's case, once he let go of the job that wasn't making him happy, he found opportunities he never would've imagined. He started working in an industry that he actually cared about. He built new relationships with people who supported his growth. And most importantly, he started living his life with **purpose**—not just for a paycheck, not just for approval, but for what God was calling him to do.

So what's that thing in your life that you're holding onto? Is it comfort? Fear? Approval? Whatever it is, it's time to lay it down.

God has something bigger, but you can't reach for it if your hands are still holding onto the old.

Before we keep going forward, let me ask you this:

1. Recognizing What to Release: What is one thing (a job, relationship, mindset, etc.) that you know you need to let go of? Be specific.

_____
_____
_____
_____
_____
_____
_____
_____
_____
_____
_____
_____
_____
_____
_____
_____
_____

2. Fear of Letting Go: What's holding you back from releasing it? What fears are keeping you from stepping into the unknown?

_____
_____
_____
_____
_____
_____
_____
_____
_____
_____
_____
_____
_____
_____
_____
_____
_____
_____
_____

3. Taking a Step of Faith: What's one action you can take today to start the process of letting go? It could be a conversation, a prayer, or even just journaling about it.

Moving Forward

Letting go of what no longer serves you is a powerful act of faith, but it's only part of the journey. Once you've made space in your life, it's time to focus on the people and relationships that surround you—and the way you see yourself.

In the next chapter, we'll dive into how your self-worth and the connections you nurture can shape your journey. Healthy relationships and a strong sense of who you are in God's eyes are the foundation for stepping into your purpose. Let's keep moving forward.

CHAPTER 3:

Relationships & Self-Worth - The Heart of Our Journey

We all know that the people in our lives play a huge role in shaping who we are, how we see ourselves, and how we move through the world. The right people can lift you up, help you grow, and remind you of your worth. But the wrong people? They can drag you down, drain your energy, and make you question your value.

Relationships are one of the most powerful influences on our lives. They're like mirrors that reflect back what we believe about ourselves. If you're surrounded by people who don't see your worth, who constantly put you down or make you feel small, it's easy to start believing that you don't deserve better. But here's the truth: **God sees you as worthy, valuable, and loved, no matter what.**

This chapter is about building relationships that reflect your God-given worth and letting go of the ones that don't. Let's dive into a few stories that show us how powerful relationships can be—and how important it is to choose them wisely.

Meet Monique: Finding Self-Worth in the Midst of Struggles

Monique is a single mom with two kids, working a part-time job and going to night school to try and build a better future. She's stretched thin, exhausted, and often feels like she's on her own. Her old friends have drifted away because they don't understand her struggles, and she's too busy to make new ones. She's caught in a cycle of survival, constantly giving to her kids, her job, her studies, and leaving nothing for herself.

One night, Monique catches a glimpse of herself in the mirror and doesn't even recognize the person staring back. She's lost her sense of self-worth, buried under the weight of everyone else's needs and expectations. She's been so focused on surviving that she's forgotten how valuable she is as a person, beyond her roles as a mom, employee, and student.

But things start to change when Monique meets a few other single moms in her night classes. They understand her struggles, and they don't judge her for being tired, for not having it all together. For the first time in a long time, Monique feels seen, understood, and valued. These new friends lift her up, remind her of her worth, and show her that she's not alone.

Monique's story teaches us that **finding our self-worth often starts with the people we surround ourselves with**. When we have people in our lives who understand, support, and encourage us, it's easier to see ourselves the way God sees us. Sometimes, we have to let go of relationships that no longer fit and seek out those who reflect our worth back to us.

Meet Aliyah: Learning to Set Boundaries with Family

Aliyah grew up in a close-knit family, where everyone was always in each other's business. She loves her family, but they have a tendency to judge her choices and make her feel like she's never quite enough. She's a people-pleaser by nature, and she often finds herself doing things just to keep the peace or make her family proud, even if it's not what she truly wants.

Recently, Aliyah has felt God calling her to pursue a career in counseling. She wants to help people who are struggling, especially young women like herself who feel trapped by others' expectations. But every time she brings it up, her family tells her that it's not a "real job," that she should aim for something more "respectable." Their words sting, and she starts to doubt her calling.

Aliyah realizes that if she's going to follow God's plan for her life, she's going to need to set boundaries. She has to stop letting her family's opinions dictate her choices. It's hard—she feels guilty for disappointing them—but she knows that honoring God's calling means valuing her own dreams and worth. Slowly, she begins to speak up for herself, to politely but firmly push back when her family tries to control her decisions.

Aliyah's story shows us that **sometimes the relationships we need to set boundaries with are the ones closest to us**. Boundaries aren't about shutting people out; they're about protecting our peace and purpose. Sometimes, following God's call means valuing our own worth over the expectations others place on us.

Lessons on Relationships & Self-Worth

From Monique's and Aliyah's stories, we can see that building healthy relationships and recognizing our self-worth go hand in hand. Here are a few key steps to help you build the kind of relationships that uplift you and remind you of your God-given worth:

1. **Seek Out Authentic Connections.** Real talk: relationships built on trust, respect, and honesty are priceless. You deserve people in your life who let you be your true self without judgment. Look for connections where you can be open about your dreams, your struggles, and your faith.
2. **Set Healthy Boundaries.** Boundaries are about protecting your peace and your purpose. It's okay to say "no" to things and people that don't align with where God is leading you. If you're around people who constantly bring you down or question your worth, it might be time to set some boundaries.
3. **Value Yourself the Way God Values You.** Your worth doesn't come from other people's opinions or approval. It comes from God, who created you with purpose. Remind yourself that you're worthy of love, respect, and support—not because of what you do, but because of who you are.

4. **Be a Source of Uplift for Others.** Relationships aren't just about what we get—they're about what we give. Be the kind of friend who listens, who encourages, who prays for others. When you uplift others, you create a space for mutual growth and support.
5. **Surround Yourself with People Who Reflect God's Love.** Find friends, mentors, and community who see your worth, who encourage you, and who remind you of God's love. These are the people who will lift you up, especially when you're struggling to see your own value.

Let me ask you this:

1. Assessing Relationships: Think about the people in your life. Which relationships make you feel valued, supported, and loved? And which ones drain you or make you question your worth?

_____
_____
_____
_____
_____
_____
_____
_____
_____
_____
_____
_____
_____
_____
_____
_____
_____

2. Evaluating Self-Worth: How do your relationships impact your sense of self-worth? Are you surrounding yourself with people who see your potential and encourage you to grow, or are you accepting less than you deserve?

3. Setting Boundaries: What boundaries do you need to set to protect your peace, your purpose, and your relationship with God? Write down one action you can take this week to prioritize your well-being.

_____
_____
_____
_____
_____
_____
_____
_____
_____
_____
_____
_____
_____
_____
_____
_____
_____
_____

Moving Forward

The relationships we keep shape so much of who we are and how we see ourselves. This chapter is a call to surround yourself with people who help you see your worth, who remind you of God's love, and who encourage you to step into your purpose. Whether it's letting go of toxic relationships, setting boundaries with well-meaning family members, or seeking out new connections that reflect your value, remember that you're worthy of relationships that lift you up.

In the next chapter, we're diving into **courage**—the courage it takes to walk away from comfort, trust in God's calling, and take bold steps forward, even when it's scary. Let's keep moving forward, together.

CHAPTER 4:

The Courage to Step Away - Your Path to the Exit Door

Let's talk about one of the biggest steps in this journey: having the courage to let go of what's comfortable and take a leap into the unknown. If you're serious about finding your exit door, then at some point, you're going to need the kind of courage that makes you say, **"I don't know what's ahead, but I trust that God has something better for me."**

Here's the thing about comfort zones: they feel safe, familiar, predictable. But comfort zones are also cages. They can keep us from growing, from stepping into our purpose, and from experiencing all that God has for us. To get to the life you were made for, you're going to have to let go of the things that are holding you back—even if they feel secure.

Let's explore a couple of stories that show us what it looks like to step away from comfort and step into faith, especially when everything around you seems uncertain.

Meet Carlos: Taking a Leap with Little Financial Security

Carlos is 35, a skilled carpenter, and a father of two. For years, he's been doing odd jobs here and there, working construction sites, fixing things up for friends, taking any gig he can find. But steady work has been hard to come by, and the bills keep piling up. He feels the weight of every late rent notice, every overdue bill, every call from a creditor. He knows he's talented, but he's also been burned by failed business ideas in the past. Part of him feels like maybe he should just keep taking what he can get and focus on making ends meet.

But Carlos has this dream—a dream to start his own small carpentry business, to create beautiful furniture and custom pieces for clients who appreciate the craft. He knows he could do it if he had the resources, but fear keeps him frozen. **"What if it doesn't work out?" "What if I can't provide for my family?" "What if I end up failing again?"**

But after a lot of prayer and conversations with his wife, Carlos feels God nudging him to take a leap of faith. He starts small, taking a few side gigs to build up his portfolio. With each project, he gains a little more confidence. And while it's hard and there are days when he doubts himself, Carlos starts to see doors open—small at first, but enough to keep him moving forward.

Carlos's story reminds us that **courage isn't about having all the answers—it's about trusting God with the unknown.** Even when the numbers don't add up, even when the future feels shaky, God calls us to take those steps of faith. Carlos doesn't have financial security, but he does have the courage to believe that God is working on his behalf, even when the path isn't fully clear.

Meet Tiana: Finding Purpose Beyond a Dead-End Job

Tiana is 24, working at a call center. She spends her days answering customer complaints, dealing with rude callers, and counting down the hours until she can clock out. She knows she's capable of so much more, but she's stuck in this job because, right now, it's what pays the bills. It's not her passion, but she tells herself she should be grateful because at least it's a job.

But Tiana feels this tug on her heart—a desire to do something that truly matters, something where she can use her creativity and connect with people in a meaningful way. She's thought about going back to school, maybe pursuing a degree in counseling, but the thought of taking on more debt scares her. Plus, she's the main provider for her family, and quitting her job seems impossible.

One night, after a particularly hard shift, Tiana breaks down and prays, **"God, if this is all there is for me, I'll keep going. But if there's something more, show me the way."** A few weeks later, a volunteer opportunity opens up at a local community center. It doesn't pay, but it allows her to work with teens and use some of the skills she's passionate about. Slowly, Tiana realizes that this experience is giving her a taste of what she truly wants to do. It's scary and uncertain, but she feels alive in a way she hasn't in years.

Tiana's story shows us that **sometimes courage means taking a step even when it doesn't make sense on paper.** She didn't quit her job right away, but she made space for something that brought her closer to her calling. Tiana learned that sometimes, finding your exit door is about trusting the small steps, letting God guide you little by little toward the bigger picture.

Lessons on Finding Courage to Step Away

Carlos and Tiana both had to step away from what felt safe in order to move toward something better. Here are a few ways you can start finding the courage to step out of your comfort zone:

1. **Visualize What's on the Other Side.** Picture the life you feel God calling you to. Imagine what it feels like to wake up with purpose, to live in alignment with your calling. Keep that vision close when fear tries to hold you back.
2. **Lean Into Faith, Not Fear.** Fear will always show up when you're stepping into something new. But when fear says, "What if it doesn't work out?" faith says, "What if it does?" Trust that God has prepared a path for you, even if you can't see it yet.
3. **Remember Past Victories.** Think back to times when you took a risk and it worked out, or when God provided for you in unexpected ways. Let those memories remind you that He's got you. He's done it before, and He'll do it again.
4. **Start Small if You Need To.** Taking a big leap doesn't mean you have to do it all at once. If you're afraid of diving in headfirst, start with something small. Take a part-time class, start a side hustle, or volunteer in an area you're passionate about. Small steps build momentum.

5. **Be Willing to Embrace Uncertainty.** The path won't always be clear, and that's okay. Sometimes, finding your exit door is about being willing to walk forward, even when you can't see the whole staircase. Embrace the unknown as a space for God to show up and surprise you.

Building a Support System for the Journey

Stepping away from comfort is hard, but you don't have to do it alone. **Surround yourself with people who believe in you, who encourage you, and who remind you of God's promises.** God often places people in our lives to guide, support, and uplift us when we're on the edge of something big.

1. **Share Your Vision.** Talk to the people closest to you about the journey you're on. Share your dreams, your goals, and your fears. When people understand what you're working toward, they can support you in a way that's meaningful.
2. **Seek Out Like-Minded People.** Find a community that's on a similar journey. Maybe it's a support group, a church ministry, or even an online group of people pursuing their passions. Being around others who "get it" will give you strength.
3. **Lean on God as Your Ultimate Support.** Remember, God is the one who planted this dream in your heart. He's with you every step of the way. Pray, seek His guidance, and trust that He'll provide what you need as you step forward.

Reflect on This:

1. Identifying Required Changes: What is one area of your life where you know you need to step out of your comfort zone? Describe it in detail.

_____
_____
_____
_____
_____
_____
_____
_____
_____
_____
_____
_____
_____
_____
_____
_____
_____

2. Confronting Fears: What fears come up when you think about making this change? Be honest with yourself. Are you afraid of failure, judgment, the unknown? List them out.

_____

_____

_____

_____

_____

_____

_____

_____

_____

_____

_____

_____

_____

_____

_____

_____

_____

3. Taking a Step of Faith: What's one small, actionable step you can take today to start moving in the direction God is calling you? Write it down, pray over it, and commit to doing it this week.

Moving Forward

The courage to step away isn't about having it all figured out. It's about trusting that God's got you, even in the uncertainty. Carlos and Tiana both found the courage to walk away from comfort because they believed that God had something better for them. And guess what? He has something better for you, too.

In the next chapter, we're diving into **embracing change** and learning how to ride the waves when life doesn't go according to plan. If you're ready to make peace with change and use it as fuel for growth, then let's keep moving forward. We're just getting started.

CHAPTER 5:

Embracing Change - Riding the Waves of Change

Change is one of those things that most of us don't exactly look forward to. Whether it's a big life shift, a career detour, or something as small as a new routine, change can feel like someone yanked the rug out from under you. And here's the kicker: change is unavoidable. It's coming, whether we're ready for it or not.

But here's the real secret—**change is where growth happens.** It's in those uncomfortable, unpredictable moments that God shapes us, challenges us, and prepares us for what's next. If you want to live the life you were called to, if you want to find your exit door, you're going to have to learn to embrace change and see it as an opportunity instead of something to fear.

Let's dive into a couple of stories that show us what it means to ride the waves of change with faith, resilience, and trust in God's timing.

Meet Jasmine: Embracing the Waiting Season After College

Jasmine just graduated from college, and like so many others, she's had a hard time landing a job in her field. She's applied to dozens of positions, gone to interviews, updated her resume, and tried everything she can think of, but the rejections keep coming. It's exhausting, and every "no" chips away at her confidence a little more. All her friends seem to be moving forward—getting jobs, moving to new cities, starting new chapters—and Jasmine feels like she's stuck in neutral.

In her mind, life was supposed to go differently. She had a plan: get the degree, land a job, start building her life. But instead, she's back at home with her parents, working a retail job she's overqualified for just to pay the bills. She feels like all her dreams are slipping further away, and she's left wondering if she's even on the right path.

One night, Jasmine breaks down and prays, **"God, if this waiting season has a purpose, please show me. I don't want to feel stuck anymore."** Slowly, she starts to realize that maybe this season is about more than just waiting—it's about growth. She begins volunteering at a local non-profit, using her skills to help others while she continues her job search. In the process, she discovers a new passion for serving people in her community, something she hadn't even considered before.

Jasmine's story reminds us that **sometimes change looks like waiting, and waiting doesn't mean you're not moving forward**. God uses those seasons of "not yet" to build our character, our resilience, and our faith. It's not easy, but when we choose to trust that God's timing is better than our own, we start to see the purpose behind the waiting.

Meet Marcus: Facing a Midlife Career Change

Marcus is in his early 50s, and he's been working at the same company for over two decades. He's good at his job, comfortable in his role, and has never really had to think about what life might look like outside of it. But then, out of nowhere, he gets the news—his position is being eliminated. He's stunned, and the thought of starting over at his age feels impossible.

Marcus had always imagined he'd retire from this job. He thought he had years left before he'd have to think about change. But now, here he is, scrolling through job listings, feeling lost and out of place in a job market that feels like it's built for younger people. Part of him feels like giving up, but deep down, he knows he can't. He still has dreams, even if they're buried under years of routine.

After a lot of prayer and reflection, Marcus starts to realize that maybe this layoff is an opportunity—a chance to pursue something that actually makes him come alive. He's always loved photography but never considered it as more than a hobby. With his wife's encouragement, Marcus decides to take a leap of faith and start a small photography business. It's scary, but it feels right. And for the first time in years, he's excited to wake up and work on something he's truly passionate about.

Marcus's story is a reminder that **change isn't bound by age**. Sometimes, God shakes up our routine to help us rediscover passions we've set aside or dreams we've buried. It's never too late to pivot, to follow a new path, or to embrace something that feels uncertain but full of possibility.

Lessons on Embracing Change

From Jasmine's and Marcus's stories, we see that change comes in many forms. Sometimes it's an unexpected shift, and sometimes it's a season of waiting. But no matter how it shows up, change is an invitation to grow, to trust, and to lean into God's timing. Here are a few ways to start embracing change, even when it feels uncomfortable:

1. **Anchor Yourself in Your Core Values.** When life is changing, it's easy to feel lost. That's when your core values become your anchor. Think about what truly matters to you—faith, family, purpose, integrity. When everything else feels uncertain, these values keep you grounded.
2. **Trust in God's Timing.** Change doesn't always happen on our schedule, and that's okay. God's timing is perfect, even when it doesn't make sense to us. Trust that if He's allowing change, He has a purpose behind it, even if you can't see it yet.
3. **Focus on What You Can Control.** In times of change, a lot of things may feel out of your hands. Instead of worrying about what you can't control, focus on what you *can*—your attitude, your actions, your faith. You can't control the waves, but you can control how you ride them.

4. **Let Go of Perfectionism.** Change is messy, and things won't always go according to plan. Let go of the idea that you have to do everything perfectly. God isn't asking for perfection; He's asking for faithfulness. Embrace the mess and trust that He's with you through it all.
5. **Pray for Wisdom and Clarity.** When you're in a season of change, don't try to navigate it alone. Lean into prayer. Ask God for wisdom, for clarity, and for the strength to keep moving forward. Prayer is your lifeline to peace and purpose when everything else feels uncertain.

Redefining Change as Growth

One of the most powerful ways to embrace change is to **reframe it as an opportunity for growth**. What if, instead of seeing change as something to fear, you started seeing it as a way to become more of the person God created you to be?

Here's how to start redefining change as growth:

1. **Ask, "What Is God Trying to Teach Me?"** Instead of focusing on why something is happening to you, start looking for what God might be teaching you *through* it. Maybe He's teaching you patience, resilience, or trust. Look for the lesson, and you'll find purpose in the change.
2. **Accept That Growth Requires Discomfort.** Real growth doesn't happen when you're comfortable. It happens when you're stretched, challenged, and pushed beyond what you think you can handle. If it feels hard, that's okay—it's a sign that you're growing.
3. **Celebrate Small Wins.** Change can feel overwhelming, so don't forget to celebrate the small victories. Every little step you take, every time you choose faith over fear, is progress. Keep track of those small wins, and let them remind you that you're moving forward.

The Role of Resilience in Embracing Change

Resilience is your secret weapon when life is shifting around you. Resilience doesn't mean that you won't feel pain, doubt, or frustration. It just means that you won't let those things stop you. Resilience is about getting back up, staying committed to your purpose, and trusting that God has got you, even when things don't make sense.

Here's how to build resilience:

1. **Remember Past Victories.** Think back to other times in your life when you faced something difficult and made it through. Let those victories remind you that you're capable, that you're strong, and that God is faithful.
2. **Focus on Your Faith.** Keeping your eyes on God, especially when things feel shaky, will help you stay strong. Let Him be your anchor. Trust in His promises, and hold on to His Word. It's your foundation when everything else feels uncertain.
3. **Take It One Day at a Time.** Change doesn't have to happen all at once. Focus on getting through today. Take it one step at a time, one prayer at a time, one moment at a time. Every day you get through, you're building resilience for the next one.

Reflect on This:

1. Personal Growth and Change: Think about a recent change in your life. What lessons did you learn from it? How did it help you grow?

_____

_____

_____

_____

_____

_____

_____

_____

_____

_____

_____

_____

_____

_____

_____

_____

_____

_____

_____

2. Attitude Toward Change: How do you typically react to change? Are you open to it, or do you find yourself resisting it? Reflect on how you can approach change with more faith and openness.

_____
_____
_____
_____
_____
_____
_____
_____
_____
_____
_____
_____
_____
_____
_____
_____
_____
_____
_____

3. Stepping Forward with Faith: Is there an area in your life right now where you know change is needed, but you've been holding back? Pray over it, ask God for strength, and commit to taking one small step this week.

Moving Forward

Embracing change isn't about knowing exactly where you're going. It's about trusting that God has a purpose for every shift, every unexpected turn, and every waiting season. Jasmine and Marcus both learned that change can be an opportunity for growth, even when it doesn't look like what they expected. And guess what? God is doing the same in your life.

In the next chapter, we'll talk about **crossing the threshold—taking that final step through your exit door and stepping boldly into the life you've been preparing for.** Let's keep moving forward, together.

CHAPTER 6:

The Exit Door Unveiled - Crossing the Threshold

Everything we've been talking about—the courage to step away, embracing change, building self-worth, and letting go of the past—it's all been leading to this moment. You're standing right in front of your exit door, open and waiting. All that's left to do is take that first, bold step through it.

Crossing the threshold is one of the hardest parts of any journey. It's like standing on the edge of a cliff, looking down at the unknown. There's excitement, but there's also fear. **What if it doesn't work out? What if I'm not ready? What if…?** These questions are natural, but here's what you need to remember: **God is already on the other side of that door, waiting for you with open arms.**

This chapter is all about that moment of decision—the point where you put everything you've learned into action, where faith meets courage, and where you finally say, "Yes, God, I'm ready." Let's look at a couple of stories of people who, despite their fears and doubts, found the strength to step through their exit doors.

Meet Shauna: Finding the Strength to Leave a Toxic Relationship

Shauna has been with her boyfriend for five years. She knows, deep down, that the relationship isn't healthy. He's controlling, emotionally distant, and has a way of making her feel like she'll never be enough. She's tried to leave before, but every time she thinks about being on her own, she feels paralyzed by fear. **What if I don't find anyone else? What if he changes? What if I can't do this on my own?**

For years, Shauna has prayed about this relationship, asking God for clarity. She knows what she needs to do, but taking that final step terrifies her. She feels trapped, like her worth is tied to someone else's opinion of her. But one night, after a difficult argument, she hears God's voice in her heart, saying, **"I created you for more than this. Step into the life I have for you."**

With that reassurance, Shauna decides it's time. She leans on her faith, knowing that God is calling her to something better, even if it means walking away from the familiar. She reaches out to a close friend, starts making plans, and gathers the courage to say goodbye. Shauna's first days alone are hard—lonely, even—but she feels a new sense of freedom, like a weight has been lifted. For the first time, she can see a future where her worth isn't defined by someone else's approval.

Shauna's story reminds us that **sometimes, crossing the threshold means choosing ourselves, choosing our worth, and believing that God has better plans for us than we have for ourselves.** It's scary to leave what's familiar, but stepping through that door was the start of her journey to true freedom.

Meet Andre: Saying Yes to a New Path Despite Fear

Andre grew up in a family where everyone followed a traditional path. His parents worked the same jobs for 30 years, saved every penny, and preached the importance of stability. Andre respects that, but deep down, he has a dream to do something different. He's passionate about music and has been producing beats on the side for years, but he's always kept it as a "hobby" because pursuing it full-time seemed reckless.

Recently, though, he's been feeling a shift. Andre's music is starting to get noticed online, and people are reaching out, asking for collaborations, even offering to pay for his work. It's exhilarating, but it's also terrifying. The thought of leaving his steady job, disappointing his parents, and risking everything on an uncertain career in music fills him with doubt. **What if I fail? What if I let everyone down?**

But after months of prayer, Andre feels a deep conviction that God is calling him to this path. He starts to realize that his passion for music isn't random—it's a gift God placed in him for a reason. With a mix of fear and excitement, Andre decides to step away from his job, cut back on his expenses, and give his music a real shot. He tells himself, **"If God put this dream in my heart, then He'll make a way."**

Andre's story shows us that **sometimes, crossing the threshold means stepping away from security and trusting that God has prepared a path, even if it's one you've never walked before.** It's about letting go of others' expectations and stepping into your own calling with faith.

Lessons on Finding Courage to Cross the Threshold

From Shauna's and Andre's stories, we see that crossing the threshold looks different for everyone. For some, it's about leaving behind a relationship or a job. For others, it's stepping away from a life that feels safe and stepping toward a calling that feels risky. No matter what your threshold looks like, here are some ways to gather the courage to take that step:

1. **Visualize What's on the Other Side.** Take a moment to imagine the life you feel God calling you to. Picture what it feels like to live in alignment with your purpose, to wake up each day excited about the life you're building. When you keep that vision in mind, the fear starts to shrink.
2. **Lean Into Faith, Not Fear.** Fear will show up, but it doesn't have to control you. When fear says, "What if it doesn't work out?" faith says, "What if it does?" Trust that God is guiding you, and that He wouldn't bring you this far just to leave you now.
3. **Remember Past Victories.** Think back to other times in your life when you took a leap of faith, even if it was a small one. Remember how God showed up for you, how things worked out,

and how you grew from that experience. Let those past victories remind you that you're stronger than you think.
4. **Focus on the First Step, Not the Entire Journey.** Sometimes we get so overwhelmed by the idea of what's ahead that we freeze up. Don't worry about the entire path right now—just focus on the first step. Take it one day at a time, one decision at a time, and let God guide you along the way.
5. **Be Willing to Embrace Uncertainty.** Stepping through the exit door is an act of faith. It means choosing to trust even when you don't have all the answers. Embrace the unknown as a space for God to show up and do something incredible in your life.

Letting Go of the Past

One of the hardest parts of crossing your exit door is leaving behind the familiar. Whether it's a relationship, a job, or simply a way of thinking, letting go of the past can feel like losing a part of yourself. But here's the thing: **you can't step into the future while clinging to the past.**

To fully embrace what God has for you, you need to create space for it. Letting go doesn't mean ignoring or forgetting where you've been; it means learning from it, honoring it, and moving forward. Here's how to start releasing the past:

1. **Reflect on the Lessons.** Take a moment to look back on the experiences, relationships, and decisions that have shaped you. What lessons did you learn? How have those experiences prepared you for where you're going?
2. **Forgive Yourself and Others.** Sometimes we hold on to the past because we're carrying guilt, shame, or resentment. If there's someone you need to forgive—including yourself—do it. Forgiveness doesn't mean condoning what happened; it just means freeing yourself from the weight of it.

3. **Choose to Move Forward.** Moving forward is an active choice. It's deciding that you're not going to let your past define your future. God has more for you, but you have to be willing to step into it.

Building a Support System for the Journey

Stepping through your exit door can feel lonely, but it doesn't have to be. **Surround yourself with people who believe in your journey, who remind you of your calling, and who encourage you to keep going.** God often uses the people around us to give us the strength we need to take that first step.

1. **Share Your Vision.** Let the people closest to you know about the journey you're on. Share your dreams, your goals, and your fears. When people understand what you're working toward, they can support you in a way that's meaningful.
2. **Connect with Like-Minded People.** Find a community that's on a similar journey. Whether it's a faith group, a mastermind, or an online community, being around people who share your values and aspirations can be incredibly empowering.
3. **Lean on God as Your Ultimate Support.** People will come and go, but God is constant. He's the one who's walking through this door with you, guiding you, and giving you strength. Lean on Him, talk to Him, and let Him be your greatest source of encouragement.

WAIT...WAIT...WAIT

Reflect on This:

1. Visualizing Your Exit Door: What does your "exit door" look like? Describe the life that awaits you once you step through it. How does it feel? Who are you becoming?

_____
_____
_____
_____
_____
_____
_____
_____
_____
_____
_____
_____
_____
_____
_____
_____
_____
_____
_____
_____

2. Steps Toward the Exit Door: What practical steps can you take to move closer to your exit door? Make a list of small, manageable actions you can start today.

3. Leaving the Past Behind: What do you need to let go of in order to fully step through your exit door? Are there past experiences, relationships, or beliefs that are holding you back? Write them down and commit to releasing them.

Moving Forward

Crossing the threshold is a powerful act of faith. It's about saying, "God, I trust You more than I trust my fear." It's choosing to believe that there's something better on the other side, even if you can't see it yet. Shauna and Andre both faced fears, doubts, and the pull to stay in what's comfortable, but they chose to step forward anyway.

In the next chapter, we'll talk about rewriting your life's narrative—how to let go of old stories, embrace new ones, and start living with intention and purpose. The journey doesn't end at the exit door; it begins there.

Let's keep moving forward. Your best life is waiting.

CHAPTER 7:

Rewriting Your Life's Narrative - Authoring Your Future

We all have stories we tell ourselves about who we are, what we're capable of, and what we deserve. Maybe you've been telling yourself that you're "not enough," or that you're always going to be "stuck." Maybe you've convinced yourself that past mistakes have disqualified you from the future you want. These narratives can become chains, keeping us locked into a life that doesn't reflect who God made us to be.

But here's the thing: **God is the ultimate author of our lives, and He has a new story waiting for you.** He's ready to help you break free from old narratives and step into a new identity, one that reflects your true worth, potential, and purpose. This chapter is all about taking the pen back and starting a new chapter, one filled with hope, growth, and faith.

Let's dive into some stories of people who learned to rewrite their life's narrative with God's help, and see what lessons we can take from their journeys.

Meet Malik: Breaking Free from the "I'm Not Smart Enough" Story

Malik grew up in a family that didn't value education. He struggled in school, and by the time he reached high school, he'd convinced himself that he just wasn't smart. Teachers told him he was "lazy" or "not motivated enough," and those words stuck with him. Over time, he started believing that he'd never be capable of more than low-paying, unfulfilling jobs. When he finally dropped out of school at 17, he felt like he'd confirmed the story he'd been telling himself his whole life: **"I'm not smart enough."**

Fast forward a few years, and Malik is working long hours at a warehouse job. He's grateful for the work, but deep down, he feels a yearning for something more. He starts going to church with a friend, and one day, the pastor's words hit him hard: **"God created each of us with unique gifts and a purpose. Don't let anyone tell you what you're worth."** Malik realizes he's been living out a narrative that was written by other people—teachers, family members, and even himself.

With a new sense of purpose, Malik decides it's time to rewrite his story. He signs up for night classes, eventually earning his GED, and even enrolls in a trade program to become an electrician. It's tough, and there are moments when the old voices of self-doubt creep back in, but Malik holds onto his faith. With God's help, he replaces the story of "I'm not smart enough" with "I am capable, and I am worthy."

Malik's story shows us that **our past doesn't have to define our future**. Just because someone once told you who you were doesn't mean you have to keep living in that story. With God's guidance, you can rewrite your narrative to reflect the truth of who you are in His eyes.

Meet Rebecca: Letting Go of Shame and Embracing Grace

Rebecca has a story she's been trying to run away from for years. When she was younger, she made choices she's not proud of—choices that left her feeling broken, ashamed, and disconnected from the person she wanted to be. She's carried this heavy weight of shame, convinced that she's "damaged goods," and unworthy of love or forgiveness.

Every time she thinks about pursuing her dreams, building relationships, or even just feeling happy, the shame creeps back in. **"Who are you to deserve a good life?"** the voice in her head taunts. She believes that because of her past, she's disqualified from the kind of future she once dreamed of.

But then, Rebecca meets a mentor at church who changes everything. Her mentor has a similar past, but she lives with freedom and joy, unburdened by shame. When Rebecca opens up to her, her mentor looks her in the eye and says, **"You are loved, and you are forgiven. God doesn't see you as damaged; He sees you as redeemed."**

With tears in her eyes, Rebecca finally starts to believe that her story isn't over. She begins to accept God's grace and let go of the shame that's kept her trapped. It's not an overnight transformation, but day by day, she rewrites her narrative. She replaces "I'm damaged goods" with "I am redeemed, loved, and worthy of a beautiful life."

Rebecca's story teaches us that **shame is a liar**. When we hold onto shame, we're holding onto a narrative that denies the power of God's grace. No matter what's in your past, God can redeem it. He can help you let go of shame and step into a story of love, grace, and new beginnings.

Lessons on Rewriting Your Life's Narrative

From Malik's and Rebecca's stories, we see that rewriting your life's narrative is all about letting go of the stories that no longer serve you. Whether it's a narrative rooted in self-doubt or shame, God is calling you to a new chapter. Here are some ways to start rewriting your story with intention and faith:

1. **Identify the Old Stories.** Take a moment to think about the narratives that have held you back. What are the lies you've believed about yourself? Maybe it's "I'm not good enough," or "I don't deserve success." Write them down so you can see them for what they are—old stories that no longer serve you.
2. **Replace Lies with Truth.** Once you've identified the lies, replace them with God's truth. Find scripture or affirmations that remind you of your worth, your purpose, and your strength. When the old narratives try to creep back in, speak these truths over yourself. Remind yourself that you are made in God's image and are worthy of every good thing.

3. **Forgive Yourself and Others.** Sometimes, the narratives we hold onto are rooted in past hurts or regrets. Forgiving yourself and others is a powerful way to break free from those stories. It doesn't mean forgetting or condoning what happened; it just means choosing to let go so you can move forward.
4. **Visualize Your New Story.** Imagine what your life looks like when you're living in alignment with God's truth. Picture yourself walking in confidence, stepping into your purpose, and letting go of the weight of old narratives. Keep this vision close as you move forward.
5. **Take Small, Brave Steps Toward Change.** Rewriting your life's narrative isn't an overnight process. It's about taking small steps every day that reflect your new story. If you're moving from "I'm not smart enough" to "I am capable," start by learning something new or taking a class. If you're moving from "I'm unworthy" to "I am loved," start by treating yourself with kindness and respect.

Embracing the Process of Transformation

Rewriting your narrative is about more than just changing your thoughts—it's about allowing God to transform your heart and mind. True transformation isn't a quick fix; it's a process, a journey of learning, growing, and unlearning. As you go through this journey, remember to be patient with yourself. God is at work in you, reshaping you into the person He created you to be.

Here's how to embrace the process of transformation:

1. **Trust God's Timing.** Transformation doesn't happen overnight, and that's okay. God knows exactly what you need and when you need it. Trust that He's working on your heart, even when you can't see immediate changes.
2. **Celebrate Your Progress.** Don't wait until you're fully "healed" or "transformed" to celebrate. Every small step, every new

thought, every act of faith is worth celebrating. Transformation is a journey, and each step forward is a victory.
3. **Surround Yourself with People Who Believe in Your New Story.** Find friends, mentors, and a community who see your potential and encourage you in your journey. People who understand your new story will remind you of it when you're tempted to slip back into the old one.
4. **Let Go of Perfectionism.** You're not expected to have it all together. God isn't asking for perfection; He's asking for faithfulness. Give yourself grace as you navigate this journey, and remember that every step you take is progress.

Let me ask you this:

1. Your Current Narrative: How would you currently describe the narrative of your life? What themes or patterns stand out? Are there any beliefs or stories you've been holding onto that no longer serve you?

2. Rewriting the Script: If you could rewrite any part of your story, what would it be and why? What new truths do you want to embrace, and what lies are you ready to let go of?

_____

_____

_____

_____

_____

_____

_____

_____

_____

_____

_____

_____

_____

_____

_____

_____

_____

_____

3. Steps Toward Your New Narrative: What small, actionable steps can you take this week to start living in alignment with your new story? Write them down and commit to taking action.

Moving Forward

Rewriting your life's narrative is about more than just changing your thoughts; it's about reclaiming your story, embracing who you are in God's eyes, and letting go of the lies that have held you back. Malik and Rebecca both chose to step out of old narratives that kept them stuck, and they found freedom in aligning with God's truth.

In the next chapter, we'll talk about **setting goals for your dream life**—how to take those new narratives and translate them into practical steps that move you closer to the life God has called you to. This journey isn't just about dreaming; it's about doing. Let's keep moving forward.

CHAPTER 8:

Setting Goals for Your Dream Life

By this point, you've confronted some old narratives, let go of things that were holding you back, and taken steps toward the life God is calling you to. Now it's time to get practical. Let's take those dreams, those visions, and those new narratives you're building and turn them into concrete goals.

Here's the thing about dreams: **a dream without a plan is just a wish.** Setting goals is how you take your dreams out of your head and start bringing them into your reality. This chapter is about taking real steps, even if they're small, toward the life you've been praying for.

We'll look at the stories of people who are learning to set goals for their dream lives, despite facing obstacles, doubts, and limited resources. You don't need to have it all figured out, but you do need to take a step. Let's see what that looks like in action.

Meet Leah: Setting Goals as a Stay-at-Home Mom

Leah is a stay-at-home mom with three young kids. She loves her family, but she often feels like she's lost a part of herself in the daily routine of diapers, dishes, and school drop-offs. Before having kids, Leah dreamed of starting her own business—something creative and flexible, like a home-based craft shop. But every time she thinks about pursuing that dream, she's overwhelmed by all the demands on her time. **"How could I possibly start something new when I barely have time for myself?"** she wonders.

But Leah realizes that this dream won't go away; it's been placed in her heart for a reason. She starts small, setting a goal to work on her business for just one hour a week. It doesn't sound like much, but she commits to it, carving out time while the kids are napping or after they go to bed. Slowly, her vision begins to take shape. She creates a few products, opens a small online shop, and starts selling her crafts. Each week, she sees a little more progress, and it motivates her to keep going.

Leah's story reminds us that **goals don't have to be big to be meaningful.** Sometimes, all you need is a little bit of consistency, a few minutes here and there, to start building momentum. Leah's goal-setting journey shows that even in a busy season, it's possible to move toward your dreams one step at a time.

Meet Jordan: Setting Goals After a Setback

Jordan used to have a stable job in the tech industry, but when his company downsized, he found himself laid off and scrambling to make ends meet. For months, he felt lost, doubting his abilities and wondering if he'd ever get back on track. He started picking up odd jobs to pay the bills, but deep down, he wanted to get back into his field, to use the skills he'd spent years developing.

After months of praying and reflecting, Jordan decides it's time to set some new goals. He makes a plan to build a portfolio and learn a new programming language that will make him more competitive in the job market. His first goal is simple: dedicate one hour each day to improving his skills. It's a small commitment, but over time, he sees real progress. Eventually, he feels confident enough to start applying for jobs again. And while it takes time, he finally lands a role that's even better than the one he lost.

Jordan's story is a reminder that **setbacks don't have to stop you from pursuing your goals**. In fact, sometimes they can push you to grow in ways you wouldn't have otherwise. By setting small, achievable goals, Jordan was able to turn his setback into a comeback.

Lessons on Setting Goals for Your Dream Life

Leah and Jordan's stories show us that goal-setting is about progress, not perfection. It's about taking small, consistent steps toward your dreams, no matter what season you're in. Here are some practical tips for setting meaningful goals that move you closer to your dream life:

1. **Start Small and Be Specific.** Big dreams can be overwhelming. Break them down into smaller, achievable goals. Instead of saying, "I want to start a business," try, "I will spend one hour a week working on my business plan." Small, specific goals are easier to stick to, and they create momentum.
2. **Set Goals That Align with Your Values.** Your goals should reflect what truly matters to you. If family time is a priority, don't set goals that require you to sacrifice that. If serving others is important, make sure your goals allow space for that. When your goals align with your values, you'll be more motivated to pursue them.
3. **Create a Realistic Timeline.** Achieving big dreams takes time, so don't rush it. Create a timeline that's realistic for your current season of life. If you're working full-time or taking care of a family, don't expect to make huge leaps overnight. Give yourself grace and trust that progress, even if it's slow, is still progress.
4. **Celebrate Small Wins.** Don't wait until you've achieved the end goal to celebrate. Every small step forward is worth acknowledging. Celebrate the little victories—they'll keep you motivated and remind you that you're on the right path.
5. **Stay Flexible and Open to God's Guidance.** Sometimes, as we start working toward our goals, God shifts our direction. Maybe He brings new opportunities or closes certain doors. Be open to His guidance, even if it means changing your plans. Trust that He knows the best path for you.

Setting "Faith Goals"

Along with practical goals, consider setting "faith goals" that help you grow spiritually and stay connected to God's purpose for your life. These aren't necessarily measurable goals, but they're commitments that keep you grounded in your faith as you pursue your dreams.

1. **Daily Time with God.** Commit to spending time with God each day—whether it's reading scripture, praying, journaling, or just sitting in His presence. This daily connection will give you strength and clarity as you work toward your goals.
2. **Trust Over Worry.** When doubts or fears creep in, make a commitment to trust God instead of worrying. Every time you feel overwhelmed, remind yourself, "God is in control, and He's guiding my steps."
3. **Seek Opportunities to Serve.** Set a goal to serve others, even if it's in a small way. Serving reminds us that our dreams are part of a bigger picture. When we focus on lifting others up, God often blesses us in unexpected ways.

The Importance of Accountability

Setting goals is one thing, but sticking to them is another. **Accountability can make all the difference.** When you have someone to encourage you, check in with you, and celebrate your wins, it's easier to stay motivated and keep moving forward.

1. **Share Your Goals with Someone You Trust.** Find a friend, family member, or mentor who supports your dreams and is willing to hold you accountable. Let them know what you're working toward, and check in with them regularly.
2. **Join a Group with Similar Goals.** If possible, find a community of people who are pursuing similar goals. This could be a church group, an online community, or a local meet-up. Being around

like-minded people who "get it" will inspire you to keep pushing forward.
3. **Set Regular Check-Ins with Yourself.** Accountability isn't just external—it's internal too. Set aside time each week to check in with yourself. Reflect on what's working, what needs adjustment, and how you're feeling about your progress. This will help you stay aligned with your goals and make necessary tweaks along the way.

Reflect on This:

1. Dream Life Goals: What are the top three goals you have for your dream life? Be specific and write them down. What do you feel God is calling you to pursue in this season?

2. Goal-Setting Plan: What actionable steps can you take to achieve these goals? Break them down into small, achievable tasks, and create a realistic timeline.

3. Accountability Partners: Who can you share your goals with? Is there someone in your life who can encourage you, hold you accountable, and celebrate your progress?

_____
_____
_____
_____
_____
_____
_____
_____
_____
_____
_____
_____
_____
_____
_____
_____

Moving Forward

Setting goals for your dream life isn't about doing it all at once. It's about taking small, faithful steps in the direction God is calling you. Leah and Jordan both set goals that felt manageable for their seasons of life, and they learned that consistency is more important than speed. Remember, God is with you every step of the way. He knows the desires of your heart, and as you align your goals with His purpose, He'll guide your journey.

In the next chapter, we'll talk about **living your dream life**—embracing fulfillment, staying present, and finding joy in every step of the journey. Because living your dream isn't just about reaching a destination; it's about savoring each moment along the way. Let's keep moving forward!

CHAPTER 9:

Living Your Dream Life - The Essence of Fulfillment

After all the soul-searching, goal-setting, and stepping through doors of opportunity, you're finally here. But here's the twist: **your dream life isn't a destination.** It's a way of living, a mindset, a daily commitment to show up as the person God created you to be.

Too often, we think fulfillment is something we'll feel *once* we reach a big goal or accomplish a lifelong dream. But fulfillment isn't a finish line—it's an everyday practice. It's about finding joy, purpose, and peace in the life you're living *right now*, not just in the life you're hoping to reach someday.

Let's look at some stories of people who've learned how to live their dream lives, not by chasing an endless list of goals, but by embracing each moment, finding gratitude in the small things, and living intentionally. Fulfillment, as you'll see, is less about what you have and more about how you choose to live each day.

Meet Rosa: Finding Fulfillment in Everyday Moments

Rosa is a retired teacher who spent her entire career pouring into her students. She loved her work, but after retiring, she found herself struggling to find purpose. For so many years, she had measured her worth by what she could give to others, and now, without the daily structure of teaching, she felt lost. **"What's left for me now?"** she wondered. She feared that her life had already peaked, that her best days were behind her.

But then, one day, Rosa has a simple moment that shifts her perspective. She's sitting outside, watching the sunrise, when she feels a profound sense of peace wash over her. In that quiet moment, she realizes that life is still filled with beauty, meaning, and purpose, even if it looks different now. She starts to focus on finding joy in the little things—spending time with family, volunteering at her church, reading books she'd always put off, and connecting with friends.

Rosa's story teaches us that **fulfillment isn't about doing more; it's about appreciating what's already in front of you.** Living your dream life isn't just about big achievements or accolades. It's about noticing the beauty in everyday moments and being grateful for the life God has given you.

Meet Anthony: Finding Purpose Through Service

Anthony is a successful business owner. On paper, he has everything he could ever want—money, respect, and influence. But despite all of this, he often feels empty, as if something is missing. He spent so many years focused on building his business and climbing the ladder that he neglected his own sense of purpose. Lately, he's been wondering if all his hard work really matters.

One day, Anthony has a conversation with a friend who volunteers at a youth mentorship program. His friend invites him to join, and though he's skeptical, Anthony agrees to give it a try. What starts as a one-time volunteer gig quickly turns into a passion. Anthony finds joy in mentoring young people, helping them navigate life, and giving back in ways that go beyond financial success.

For the first time in years, Anthony feels a sense of purpose that fills the emptiness he couldn't seem to shake. He realizes that fulfillment isn't about how much he can accomplish for himself—it's about using his gifts to uplift others. Anthony's story shows us that **true fulfillment comes from serving and pouring into others**. When we give of ourselves, we often find that what we gain in return is far greater than what we gave.

Lessons on Living a Fulfilled Life

Rosa and Anthony's stories teach us that living a fulfilled life is about shifting our focus from "getting" to "being." It's about recognizing that fulfillment is found in gratitude, presence, and purpose. Here are some ways you can start living your dream life, right here and now:

1. **Practice Gratitude Daily.** Fulfillment starts with gratitude. Take a few moments each day to thank God for what you have right now. This could be as simple as appreciating a warm meal, a kind word from a friend, or the beauty of nature. Gratitude shifts your focus from what's missing to what's already here.
2. **Find Joy in the Present Moment.** It's easy to get so caught up in future goals that you forget to enjoy the present. Make it a habit to savor the little things—the sound of laughter, a good conversation, the warmth of sunlight on your face. Living your dream life means being fully present in the life you're living today.
3. **Use Your Gifts to Serve Others.** There's a special kind of fulfillment that comes from using your talents to make a difference in someone else's life. Look for ways to give back, whether it's through mentoring, volunteering, or simply showing kindness. When you focus on lifting others, you often find that your own sense of purpose grows.
4. **Celebrate the Journey, Not Just the Destination.** Goals are important, but don't forget to celebrate the progress you're making along the way. Each step, each small win, is part of your journey. Take time to appreciate how far you've come and to honor the work you're putting in.
5. **Stay Connected to God's Vision for Your Life.** Fulfillment comes from aligning your life with God's purpose. Spend time with Him, seek His guidance, and ask Him to reveal the steps He wants you to take. When you walk in alignment with God's will, you'll feel a peace that goes beyond anything this world can offer.

Living with Intention

Living your dream life isn't about waiting for something to happen. It's about making intentional choices every day that align with your purpose, values, and faith. Here's how to live with intention:

1. **Set Daily Intentions.** Each morning, set an intention for the day. This could be something like, "Today, I'm going to focus on gratitude," or "Today, I will speak kindly to myself." Setting an intention helps you live each day purposefully and keeps you aligned with your goals.
2. **Align Your Actions with Your Values.** Take a moment to think about what truly matters to you. If family is important, make time for them. If growth is a priority, spend time learning. When your actions align with your values, you'll feel a greater sense of fulfillment.
3. **Prioritize Rest and Self-Care.** Living your dream life doesn't mean you have to be constantly busy. Rest is just as important as action. Make time to recharge, care for your body, mind, and spirit, and give yourself grace on the days when you need to slow down.
4. **Reflect and Reevaluate.** Take time to regularly reflect on your life. Are you moving in the direction you want to go? Are your goals and actions still aligned with your purpose? Life changes, and it's okay to adjust your path as you go.
5. **Stay Open to God's Surprises.** Sometimes, God's plan for your life is different from your own. Be open to the unexpected and trust that His vision is always better. Fulfillment often comes when we surrender our own plans and allow God to lead.

Reflect on This:

1. Defining Your Dream Life: What does living your dream life mean to you? Think beyond material success—what kind of person do you want to be? How do you want to feel each day?

_____

_____

_____

_____

_____

_____

_____

_____

_____

_____

_____

_____

_____

_____

_____

_____

2. Barriers to Fulfillment: What obstacles are currently in the way of living your dream life? Are there habits, mindsets, or external factors that hold you back from feeling fulfilled?

_____
_____
_____
_____
_____
_____
_____
_____
_____
_____
_____
_____
_____
_____
_____
_____
_____

3. Living with Purpose: How can you bring more intention into your daily life? What small changes can you make today to align more closely with your values and purpose?

Moving Forward

Living your dream life isn't about achieving everything you've ever wanted. It's about learning to be grateful, present, and purposeful in the life God has already given you. Rosa and Anthony both discovered that true fulfillment isn't found in accolades or status, but in gratitude, service, and connection. When you live with intention, rooted in faith, you'll find that your life feels richer, more meaningful, and full of joy.

In the final chapter, we'll talk about **reflecting on your journey**—looking back on where you've been, celebrating how far you've come, and staying committed to living your purpose. This journey doesn't end here; it's just the beginning. Let's keep moving forward.

CHAPTER 10:

Beyond the Exit Door – Reflecting on Your Journey

Here you are, standing on the other side of your exit door. You've been through the highs, the lows, the breakthroughs, and the setbacks. You've taken bold steps, faced your fears, rewritten your story, and started building a life that's in line with who God made you to be. Now, it's time to pause, look back, and give thanks for how far you've come.

This chapter is about reflection, about honoring the journey you've been on. It's about celebrating the victories, big and small, and recognizing the person you've become along the way. But it's also about looking forward, knowing that this journey doesn't end here. Finding your exit door is only the beginning. The real adventure is in what comes next—in continuing to live with purpose, to grow, and to inspire others to do the same.

Let's dive into some stories of people who have crossed their own exit doors and learned to embrace the journey. Their stories show us that reflection isn't just about looking back; it's about using what you've learned to keep moving forward.

Meet Dana: Celebrating Growth and Embracing New Chapters

Dana is a single mom who spent years feeling like she was just trying to survive. Between raising her kids, working multiple jobs, and dealing with the financial stress of being on her own, Dana often felt overwhelmed and exhausted. But along the way, she found her exit door. She began to lean on God, trust His guidance, and take small steps to build a better life for herself and her family.

Now, as she stands on the other side, she feels a deep sense of gratitude—not just for what she's achieved, but for the strength she discovered within herself. Looking back, she realizes that every struggle, every late night, and every hard decision helped her grow into the resilient, faith-filled woman she is today. She's proud of the journey, and she knows that she's capable of facing whatever comes next.

Dana's story reminds us that **reflection is about celebrating how far we've come**. It's about recognizing the strength we've gained, the lessons we've learned, and the person we've become. Dana's journey isn't over; she knows there will be new challenges ahead, but now she has the confidence to face them, knowing that God is with her.

Meet Eli: Using His Journey to Inspire Others

Eli grew up in a tough neighborhood where opportunities were limited and success stories were rare. He spent years feeling stuck, convinced that he was destined for a life of struggle. But through faith, mentorship, and hard work, Eli found his way out. He built a career, found stability, and started living with a sense of purpose he never thought possible.

Now, Eli is dedicated to giving back. He mentors young men in his community, sharing his story and encouraging them to dream bigger. He reminds them that they, too, can find their exit doors and create a new path for themselves. **"If I can do it, so can you,"** he tells them. For Eli, reflecting on his journey isn't just about gratitude; it's about using his experiences to inspire others.

Eli's story shows us that **our journeys aren't just for us—they're for others, too.** When we share our struggles, our breakthroughs, and our victories, we give others hope. We show them what's possible, and we remind them that they're not alone on their journey.

Lessons on Reflecting and Moving Forward

From Dana's and Eli's stories, we see that reflection is about more than just looking back. It's about celebrating, learning, and using what you've gained to keep moving forward. Here are some ways to embrace reflection and let it fuel your journey:

1. **Celebrate Every Victory, Big and Small.** Reflection is about honoring all the steps you've taken, not just the big milestones. Every small win, every hard choice, every act of faith is worth celebrating. Take time to acknowledge and be grateful for each moment that brought you to where you are.
2. **Acknowledge the Hard Times, Too.** Your journey likely had its fair share of struggles and setbacks. Don't gloss over them. Recognize the strength, resilience, and growth that came from those moments. Often, the hardest times are what prepare us for the biggest blessings.
3. **Look for Patterns and Lessons.** As you reflect, look for patterns in your journey. Are there recurring themes, lessons, or areas where you've consistently grown? Recognizing these patterns can give you clarity on the unique purpose God has for your life and help you continue moving forward with intention.
4. **Give Thanks and Praise to God.** Remember that you didn't do this alone. God has been with you every step of the way, guiding, supporting, and strengthening you. Take time to thank Him for His presence in your journey, for the doors He opened, and even for the doors He closed.
5. **Share Your Story.** Your story has the power to inspire and uplift others. Don't keep it to yourself. Whether it's through a conversation, a blog post, social media, or mentoring someone, find ways to share what you've learned. When you open up, you create a space for others to find hope, encouragement, and faith.

Keeping Your Journey Alive

Crossing your exit door doesn't mean the journey is over. Living a life of purpose is a lifelong commitment to growth, faith, and intentionality. Here's how to keep the lessons from your journey alive as you move forward:

1. **Continue Setting New Goals.** Don't stop dreaming and setting goals just because you've reached a milestone. God has more in store for you. Keep seeking His guidance, keep growing, and keep moving toward the next chapter He has for you.
2. **Embrace Lifelong Learning.** Every season of life has new lessons to teach. Stay open to learning, whether it's through experiences, people, or God's word. Growth is a continuous journey, and each lesson brings you closer to the person God created you to be.
3. **Stay Connected to Your "Why."** Remember the reasons you started this journey—the dreams, the calling, the purpose that inspired you. Keep that "why" close to your heart. Let it be the fuel that keeps you moving forward, even when the path gets challenging.
4. **Serve and Uplift Others.** As you continue on your journey, make it a priority to give back. Look for ways to encourage, mentor, or support others who are searching for their own exit doors. When you lift others up, you're building a legacy that goes beyond your own life.
5. **Trust God's Ongoing Plan.** Your journey isn't over, and neither is God's work in your life. Trust that He has new doors to open, new paths to explore, and new dreams to pursue. Keep walking in faith, knowing that He's guiding you every step of the way.

Reflect on This:

1. Key Takeaways: What are the key lessons you've learned from this journey? Write down the insights, growth moments, and truths that have shaped you.

_____
_____
_____
_____
_____
_____
_____
_____
_____
_____
_____
_____
_____
_____
_____
_____

2. Sharing Your Story: How can you use your experiences to inspire and uplift others? Think of ways you can share what you've learned, whether through mentoring, volunteering, or simply being open about your journey.

_____

_____

_____

_____

_____

_____

_____

_____

_____

_____

_____

_____

_____

_____

_____

_____

_____

_____

3. Looking Forward: As you continue on this journey, what new dreams or goals do you have? How will you keep moving forward with purpose and faith?

Beyond the Exit Door

YOU DID IT!!! You've walked through the exit door, stepped into a life aligned with your purpose, and embraced a journey of faith, growth, and fulfillment. And while you may be standing on the other side, this isn't the end—it's just the beginning.

Every step you've taken has prepared you for what comes next. The lessons, the strength, and the resilience you've gained will carry you forward. So as you move beyond this chapter, keep walking in faith, keep trusting God, and keep choosing to live with purpose.

The journey will continue, with new doors to open, new paths to explore, and new dreams to pursue. And as you walk forward, remember that you're not just living for yourself. Your story is a light for others, a beacon of hope, and a reminder of what's possible.

Go out there and live the life you were created for. Be bold, be kind, be faithful. Share your story, uplift others, and never stop growing. **Your journey is far from over, and the best is yet to come.**

Note to You

As you close this book, remember that you are equipped, you are worthy, and you are capable of living your dream life. God has already placed everything you need within you. Walk forward with confidence, knowing that you're on a path that's uniquely yours—a path that's guided by faith, purpose, and God's unwavering love.

Thank you for taking this journey. Now, go out and live it.

A Prayer for You

Dear God,

Thank You for every person reading this book, for their courage to seek, to grow, and to step into the life You've called them to. I lift them up to You, asking that You continue to guide their steps, strengthen their faith, and fill them with peace and confidence as they move forward. Remind them that they are never alone—that You are with them every step of the way, holding them, encouraging them, and lighting their path.

Help them to see themselves through Your eyes, to know that they are loved, chosen, and capable. When doubt or fear tries to creep in, let them feel Your presence and Your promise that You have a plan for their lives—a plan filled with hope and a future. Give them the courage to keep moving forward, to embrace new challenges, and to live with purpose, no matter what comes their way.

Lord, may their lives be a light to others. May they inspire, uplift, and bring hope to those around them. Let their journey be a testimony to Your faithfulness and a reminder that with You, all things are possible.

In Jesus' name, Amen.

www.ingramcontent.com/pod-product-compliance
Lightning Source LLC
Chambersburg PA
CBHW050247010526
44107CB00003B/227